Introduction

When I first started writing in 1999, I did not know anyone or anything about writing. All I knew is I had a story I wanted to tell, so like most first time writers I sat down at my computer and started typing my great American novel. I had been in Corporate America for twenty-three years and all I knew was business. A book came to me one night in my sleep, it was so vivid that the next morning I got up and wrote everything down on a pad and laid it on my office desk. I was never what I called a 'closet writer' someone who really wants to write, but has not come out into the world yet to become a writer. I was always an avid reader, but I never had the desire to write. At the same time I did not realize I had become burned-out with my career and was unhappy until I started crying and could not stop. I started playing around with writing a book, because I had lost my interest in business. After losing my only sister in a car accident in 2000, I buried myself into the book because I was mourning. When I finished the book, I realized right then I wanted to become a writer. I closed my business with my business partner and started on a new career as a professional writer.

After leaving a corporate career, with business being such a part of who I was, I knew it had to be a business side to writing and those books just do not appear on the shelf in book stores overnight. I started on my journey to find out about the world of writing. The first thing I discovered that not only was writing a business, but one of the most serious businesses around. I had fifty million questions. How do I get published? How long does it take to get a book into a book store? Do I need an agent or should I self-publish? How do I get paid once my book is published? Where do I send my manuscript once I finish it and how will I know it's right?

These were just some of the questions I had about getting started in the career as a professional writer. I sent myself back to school, the school of the Public Library and Internet. I read everything I could get my hands on about writing and how to get published. I discovered that I wanted an agent to represent me and I was not going to get a book deal overnight. I knew I had to make some money, because I was not working anymore since I had walked away from my corporate career to become a writer. That's when I discovered freelance writing. I could write articles on different subjects and get paid quickly for it.

That's also when I started studying about freelance writing and decided to not only try to get the book published through an agent, but start a career as a freelancer to get paid right away. I found an agent who did like my story, but did not like the way I had wrote the book. My dialogue and visual aid was not strong and the format of the book was incorrect. I had a great story, but not a good book. That's when I learned it is a lot to this writing thing, which most new writers do not know or understand in the beginning. I worked on the book and even started working on a second book, until my path went into a different direction of teaching writing.

When I took writing class myself, the instructor, who happen to be one of Stephen King editors and I started talking and he suggested I teach a freelance writing class through the Continued Education Department at The University of Memphis. I had been a trainer in corporate and at the time of the class I had published over fifty articles. I looked into what he suggested and had the opportunity to teach a freelance writing class in 2004 at The University of Memphis. I fell in love with teaching about writing and realized all the data I had on writing from the previous years when I was studying the field came into place for teaching.

Coming home one night from class, I realized there in Memphis they only had classes on writing every once in awhile through the University and what do writers there do when they miss that class, or writing classes are not running for that semester? That's when I developed the company Writing4Success. I knew there had to be other people like me in the city who wanted to write, but did not know how to get started, how to get their work published or understand the business side of writing. I developed the company Writing4Success PR and Marketing for a literary connection to help writers become successful published writers. As I tell every student who has taken a class from me; I've been there, I've been in your shoes of not knowing anyone in the industry or what to do. I had no mentor or guidance for my writing and that is why I developed the company for the writer in you.

The company went in a new direction after only teaching writing classes for awhile. I started an Editing Service, because once I finished working with writers on how to write their books, I could edit their work.

This worked out well because I was familiar already with the writer's work, so they felt comfortable in letting me do the editing. Then I started consulting writers on different areas of writing from publishing to book concept, to coaching some writers to actually write. Next I started doing Public Relations for authors when their books were published and I fell in love with PR and Marketing for writers. Public Relations and Marketing is the one area that most writers do not think about or a topic that is not discussed that much among writers. It is one of the most important areas for a writer, without it no one will know you have written a book and you will not become an established published writer.

And now, I have written this book as a guide for new and old writers on the importance of Public Relations and Marketing for writers. You will understand why you need it, along with what to look for and expect when you use that source. This book is not only a step by step guide on the four main tools for Public Relations and Marketing that a writer need, but this book is your friend, because it will tell you how to do your own Public Relations and Marketing.

This book is for when you have published a book; whether you go through a publishing house or you self-published, you will know what to do after publication to make your book a success. I would love to have each and everyone of you in my office for a consulting session or at a writer's conference when I'm speaking on PR and Marketing for writers, but since I cannot, I decided to bring the consulting session and speaking engagements to you through this book. The Four Steps of Public Relations and Marketing for Writers is a book of my consulting sessions, speaking engagements and tips that I have shared with many upcoming writers. I cannot guarantee anyone that you will be on the New York Bestseller list, but I can guarantee that your writing will be known and you will become a success as a writer. Like my former company Writing4Success PR and Marketing and my current company Rose Walker Writing Consultants, my book The Four Steps of Public Relations and Marketing for Writers is for the writer that is in each and every one of you. Enjoy.

Chapter One

Why Writers Need Public Relations and Marketing

Public Relations and Marketing is something that is not discussed that often in the field of writing. It is an area that has been overlooked, but it is the main key to becoming a successful author. Every writer, no matter what you are writing about has to do marketing to locate a place to publish their work. If you are an author you will have to find an agent or a publishing house and if you self-published, you will have to find a publisher to print your book before someone can read it.

Any of these steps are marketing. This becomes an automatic step for every writer, but once that book is published most writers do not think about the PR and Marketing it takes to reach a variety of people and to keep their name and the book out in the public. Once your book is in print most writers think their job is done. This is only the beginning, your book might be in print and family, friends and co-workers know you have written a book, but what about the rest of the world?

When most writers are in the process of writing their books, all they can think about is finishing the book and getting it published. They can't wait for everyone to read it and all writers daydream of sitting at Barnes and Noble signing their book, and seeing it has made number one on the bestseller list. What writers do not think about is how they end up sitting at a table conducting a book signing.

They never think about why and how all those people who are standing in line for them to sign their book, or what made it get on the bestseller list that they are now cutting that clip out of the newspaper for their own personal scrape book. It just does not happen without something or someone making it happens. That something is Public Relations and Marketing for that book. The book is finished and now is in print and ready for the world, but the world will not know it exist if something is not done to put it out there into the world.

That's when Public Relations and Marketing comes into play; it is the missing link for most writers to promote and become profitable from their work. Public Relations is exactly what it sounds like, making the public aware you have something for them. Marketing is getting your product out to the public.

For a writer your product is your book and that book has to be made aware of to the public. PR and Marketing is an area that most people relate to with corporations and entertainers, because they are the ones that marketing campaigns are usually designed for and a Publicist is what most entertainers have to help them promote their projects. A writer needs the same thing for their books. Once you have written and published a book, every writer needs to think about the future of that book. How many people can they reach to read their work and how to develop a clientele for their books for that clientele to be waiting for the next one? Marketing your book the right way will reach people everywhere and you will develop a fan base along the way.

Writers spend so much time on actually writing the book and finding a way to get it in print, whether they go through a publishing house or now days they just pay for it themselves by self-publishing. What happens after all the hours and all the hard work that you put into your book, what do you do next? Next is something most writers do not think about, next is getting that book out there along with who you are as the author.

It is very important for every writer in the beginning of their career to establish themselves and their work to keep the public knowing who they are and wanting that book, along with cannot be waiting for the next one. That's why Public Relations and Marketing is such an important component of every writer's career. With the right PR and Marketing it can make that happen.

These days there are two ways a writer can get their work published: a publishing house or to self-publish. When published through a large publishing house, you will have the publicity department to work with you on marketing your book and set up some of your book signings. But even then, you should still have ideas about doing your own PR and Marketing, because the publisher's publicity department will do only so much. If you are self-published, once that book is printed what do you do next? You give out copies to your friends, sell some copies to your co-workers and the rest just sit in your house. Why waste your time and money if you are not going to go all the way to get the book out in the world? There is no way around it: as a writer, if you want your book to be read, you need Public Relations and Marketing.

You have a great book that you have a message that you want to share. You have to get your baby out there in the world.

I had a client that I worked with for years on his book and once it was finished he decided he was going to publish it himself. I told him that's great and then I asked the question, then what? He looked confused at that question; because he felt he was through. He had spent years writing and I had edited and edited his book and now all that was left was to get it into print. I told him once you get it printed, who was going to read it if they do not know it exist.

You have spent a lot of time and money on this book. You have paid me for classes and consulting sessions, along with editing fees and now you are going to spend a big sum of money to have it printed. Don't you think everyone should know about the book? Don't you want more than family, friends and co-workers to read the book? If this book does not have any Public Relations and Marketing it will not reach people. You only have so many people in your family, a certain amount of friends in your life and only the co-workers that you work with on your job.

I told him do not be one of the many writers who books have just sat around after it was in print and let all your hard work and money go down the drain. He looked at me with such a surprise look, that I had to laugh. He said the whole time he was writing the book all he wanted to do was to finish it and see it in print, he never though about the future of the book.

He is not alone. Most writers do not think about the future of their books and how and what to do to make sure that book even has a future. The writer's process is to just get it finish and printed into a book form, once that's done they feel their job is completed. Wrong.

That's when your job really begins, you the writer is responsible for getting your book out there. You can hire someone professional to do it, or try to do it yourself. Doing it yourself you will find that it can be a full-time job and you are left no time to write, if you do not know how to do it the right way where it will not interfere with your writing.

This author had a whole new outlook about things after we finished our consulting session that day, because these were things that he never thought about concerning his book.

I laid out a one year plan for the book from the day it went to print. He asked why I didn't start the plan after the book was published.

I explained to him that you do not have to wait until your booked is published to start a Public Relations campaign, that once your book go to print that's when your campaign should start. A good publicist will start while your book is being printed so when it does come out, they are ready to kick your book campaign off.

I once had a dinner meeting with an author who has written several books and they all are self-published books, so they did all the Marketing and PR for their own books. They booked all their speaking engagements and any conferences they attended. They told me over dinner; it was beginning to be too much. They had a new book they wanted to start on, but marketing the old books and trying to book speaking engagements all over the country, left them with no time to write.

This author was feeling very overwhelm and really sad that they could not spend a lot of time on their new book that they wanted to write.

I told them that were one of the problems I was seeing with a lot of writers, especially brand new ones, they cannot handle the PR and Marketing and write at the same time, but you have to have that PR and Marketing for the book to become a success. I suggested to them to look at the process this way.

That book is your baby and just like a child that you prepare for to send them to one of the best schools by doing research on that school for their future, it's the same thing with your book. You want the best for your book and you have to prepare for its future. A book is something that will be around forever and it can reach the hands of people all across the world. Your book doesn't have to just circulate only where you live, it can be everywhere. To get your book everywhere, you need the right Public Relations and Marketing. Public Relations and Marketing can be a full-time job that professionals do.

Designing Public Relations and Marketing campaigns take a lot of time and a lot of leg work to make it work. Each book that is written is special and need special attention for that book to become a winner. That's why there are four tools in Public Relations and Marketing that are used to promote, market, and sell your books.

Those main four tools needed for PR and Marketing are: a Publicist, Media Kit, Marketing Campaign and Book Promotion Items. These four tools will help you to have the publicity and promote your book, along with making profits. The goal to writing any book is to share some type of message with people about what you have written. Publicity will let them know the book exists; promotion is getting out in the public as an author with your book and making profits comes from selling a large quantity of books.

Implementing the four tools of Public Relations and Marketing will allow you to do that. Not using these tools is one of the biggest mistakes that many authors make, especially brand new authors.

A newly published author is only going to be excited that their first book is finally in print and do not think about how they are going to promote, publicize, or make money from their new book. Do they think of hiring a Publicist, and making sure they have a marketing campaign specifically designed for their book? No. They only know it's finished, it's in print and now they can say they are an author.

You have to remember there are so many new titles published every year, and it can be difficult to compete, and capture the attention of the reading public without PR and Marketing for your book. Writers sometimes feel their books will sell themselves, but this is not true. A successful selling author has the right tools that have made them become successful.

They know once they finish the writing and publishing part, it's time for the business end to be put into place. In the very beginning the creative part is fun, you're getting to create a story and that can be very exciting. Next a little of the work starts when you have to edit and do rewrites, then finding somewhere or someone to publish it can become a job within it self. Once it is finally published you have to get into full business mode and that's when the business end of writing comes into place.

Public Relations and Marketing is the business end of writing. Without it a writer will not be known as an author; people will not read your work, and you will not sell a large amount of books. Now that anyone can have their books printed because of self-publishing, it is doubly important for writers to have PR and Marketing for their books.

As an independent author your work may not be noticed by the major distributors who are the backbone of the publishing industry. There are not many major bookstores that will placed your books into their book stores if they are not carried by major distributors and that's why you need a marketing plan.

By having a professional marketing campaign and a Publicist to create that campaign to make sure it is carried through, you stand a better chance of being in major bookstores. The goal for any writer is to have book signings, do a book tour, and create a following for their books, along with making money. This can all be accomplished with PR and Marketing.

When a writer takes on the job of doing the Marketing and PR themselves, they usually short change their writing career. They do not have the contacts the professional have and most importantly it takes away from their writing. You can spend days on the phone, going to venues and writing press releases for your book, which will leave very little time to write the next book. When I work with clients for the first time, I always ask them where they want to go with their book.

Is this just a one time book, because they had this great story they wanted to share or is this just the beginning and they want to become a professional writer? It makes a difference, because a one time book will not need a major PR and Marketing campaign. They want people to read the book, but they do not have to stay out in the public since it will not be anymore books. If you want a career as a writer your campaign need to be designed to keeping your name and book in the public, because you want them waiting for the next one.

Just like you write a book that can become a saga, you leave the door open for some of the characters in that book to have a story of their own; you do the same thing with Marketing and PR for your book by making the reader want your next book.

It is a very serious area for a writer, which most writers do not think about or decide they need. But your book needs PR and Marketing to get it into the hands of a variety of people instead of just your close circuit of people. You sell more books and you can build a cliental that is waiting for your next book. You can do a small book signing at home or you can have a major book signing at several book stores.

At home you called everyone you know to come over, in a book store your Publicist will have arranged for the book signing and did the advertising for it also, which will have people there that you know and do not know. You will reach more people going through a Publicist than just having family friends over at your home.

The most important thing you will have when doing PR and Marketing is for your book to exist. So many writers publish books and know one know they exist. It is very common in these days and times, because so many writers are paying to have their books printed up themselves and people do not know they have even written a book, because they have no avenue in getting that book out there.

When doing speaking engagements on PR and Marketing I ask how many writers have a Publicist or work with a firm to design them a marketing campaign for their books, usually no one raises their hands. I have found most writers do not hire anyone or specifically design a campaign themselves for their book.

They might make a few phone calls to a couple of places to see if they can have a book signing there, but they do not have a concrete plan on doing a certain amount of book signings per month, speaking at organizations, participating at several book fairs and having a list of TV and radio talk shows that they plan to be on to promote their book. These are some of the things a professional Publicist will do for you and more.

Even though writing is a career that you do all alone, and you don't need a staff or a big fancy office, the end result is a product that you want out there. Like any other product, it has to be marketed and you do need Public Relations to achieve that. Do not short change your book, whether you go through a publishing house or you publish it yourself. A writer has a message to share and in order for that message to be shared; your book has to be available. Most importantly, people have to know you have written that book before they can get your message.

How does this all start? It starts when you get a Publicist; they create your media kit and a marketing campaign, and help you to develop book promotion items for your books.

In this book we will cover the Publicist which is where it all starts with and what a Publicist can do for you. Along with what you, the writer should look for when working with a Publicist. After the Publicist I will discuss the Media Kit, from why you need it and what's in it. Then we will get into the Marketing Campaign of how to design one and what to expect when someone else design a campaign for you. And last, Book Promotion Items that will have your name and your book out there in the public eye, with the different promotional ideas you can use. I will also talk about the difference in book signings and a book party and why both can help you. Of course we will talk about speaking engagements, promoting online and the best way to get your book out there through radio, TV and print. The most important thing we will discuss is how can you do all this yourself and still have the time to write.

Most new writers do not have the funds in the beginning of their career to go out and hire a Publicist to design a Public Relations and Marketing campaign for their book. Especially if you have self-published your book, the money you put into paying to have it printed will sometimes leave you without a cash flow for anything else.

Of course you will not do a campaign like a professional Publicist, but there are ways that you can design your own campaign that can be successful and still allow you the time to write.

The key to doing your own Public Relations and Marketing is to think of it as a job. As a matter of fact… you should think of it as a part-time job. That means you should set some hours as if you were going to be going to work. I suggest that you spend Mondays and Fridays as your full-time days of writing and do your Public Relations and Marketing Tuesday, Wednesday, and Thursday from 9:00am to 1:00pm and after 1:00pm spend the rest of the day writing.

Those three days and those times of the day are good for handling business and making business phone calls. Remember you need to talk to business people and business companies, so you need their hours to make it work. Once you put on your PR hat, you have to think and act like a professional Publicist in order to succeed in your Public Relations and marketing campaigns.

Once a writer understands how Public Relations and Marketing can advance their careers, and start using these tools, they are on their way to prosperity.

When you think about the years it took to write the book and the money some writers invest to get their books in print, you do not want that time or money to go to waste. Why do writers need Public Relations and Marketing? It's simple: you wrote it and now you want someone to read it. So let's get started…and it all starts with one person: The Publicist.

Chapter Two

The Publicist

Who cares about your published book as much as you do: Your Publicist? A Publicist is a professional in the business of generating publicity for your book, along with creating and developing a marketing plan, and will be the liaison between the author and the media. A good Publicist will focus on generating media attention on your book and do a marketing campaign that will keep you and your book circulating. You want to make sure they can do a marketing campaign and not just media buzz, because you need them both. They are there to provide insight and advice on the publishing industry, along with telling you the commercial stages and development of your book.

A Publicist becomes your best friend as writer, because you and this person will communicate all the time, and actually if and when you do book tours your Publicist sometimes goes with you. This means if you have a Publicist, beside that person working for you to get your book out there, you need to make sure the two of you can get along with each other personally.

You should also interview several Publicists before making a decision on who you want to work with, because not only do you need to know they can do the job you need and want, but the two of you can work together. So why do you need one? A Publicist will promote and keep your name and your book out in the public for you to become a successful author.

When most people think about having a Publicist, they think about movie stars; their Publicist having booked them in everywhere to talk about their new movie. Whenever a new movie premiers you see the stars of that movie on every talk show; their Publicist is keeping their names out in the public so everyone will go to see that movie. But we hardly ever relate a Publicist to a writer. A writer needs the same thing when their book premiers. They need someone to book them on every television and radio show to talk about their new book coming out, so everyone will go buy their book to read it. Writers need a Publicist, just like an entertainer needs one.

Having a Publicist is one of the major tools any writer can have for their career. Just like you have that computer to write those words on, you need publicity for those words and with the right person to help make sure someone will read them.

When one of my clients had finally finished their book and had it self-published, we had a meeting and they wanted to know what do they do next? I had consulted on the book and did the editing, so they asked could I still work with them, but they didn't know what I could do with them now that they had finished and published their book. I suggested I could become their Publicist to help promote the book. Not really understanding what a Publicist could do for them, I explain what I would do and then I asked them one question "Now that the book is in print, what are your plans for the book?" They stared into space for about five minutes, before realizing they did not have a plan for their book. I found that most writers do not think about that next step after publishing their work. That's when a Publicist really comes into play to promote and market your newly published book. As I explain to the writer, I will start working a marketing campaign right now for the book and not after it's printed.

I will design a marketing campaign on their book subject and as a self-published book. Every Publicist should design a marketing campaign on a personal level, because each book is different. This particular book was romance with a strong female lead that actually walked away from love.

The character was very career orientated and I kept that in mind when designing their book campaign. The author niche was a romance novel that the lead female character did not end up with the lead male character, so I focus on marketing the book as a romance novel that had a twist at the end. Most romance novels always end up happily ever after and this one did not. This was a great marketing tool, because it was such a twist for a romantic novel.

A Publicist has to design campaigns to fit your book storyline, but also the campaign should be designed on how your book is published. If going through a publishing house or self-published the campaigns can be totally different. When publishing through a publishing house you will have a PR representative that will work with you to promote your new book, but they might not give you full attention because you are a brand new author and they tend to focus on the more established authors that they know will produce. I am not saying they won't work with you and do a good job; you just have to keep in mind that this is your first book and they tend to do more elaborate campaigns with established authors.

That's why you should make sure you have someone that will work with and for you. Do not depend on the publishing house Publicist to launch your career, hire your own Publicist.

A self-published author definitely needs to hire a Publicist to promote and guide them on how to get their book out there to reach the public. Once you pay to have your book printed, everything else is left up to you. You are responsible for marketing your own book and that is a job within itself. Hiring a Publicist as a self-published author will not only get your book out in the public to reach more people, but it frees you up from that end of the business side.

Whether you self-publish or go through a publishing house using a Publicist is for your benefit, to get you and your book out there and free up your time to write. There are more people to support you getting your book out there when you do go through a publishing house, but self-published authors are really on their own. Everything has to be handled as if you are published through a publishing house, because you want that same response as an author who does go through a publishing house who gets all that support.

Most writers want to spend most of their time writing and not dealing with the business side of writing. That's find…but just like any other career that you would have, you would deal with the business side of it to become a success in your career. It's the same thing with your writing, in order to be a successful writer you have to know and understand all the outs and ends of the business side of writing, along with promotion is a very important part of that business side to become a success There are certain people in the writing world that can help you get to that level and a Publicist is one of them. They are usually very dedicated to what you have written and have a passion for your story just as much as you do. Having that passion for your story is what will motivate that Publicist to work hard to get it out to everyone to read your book.

Yes it's your career, but if you do not have those skills to promote your book, than hire someone who will. To make money you have to spend money.

Investing in a Publicist will be worth every dime that you spend, because you will get it all back. The Publicist goal is to make your book known to the public, which will in return produce sales and sales will produce cash.

The goal when you write a book is for someone to read it, the reward is making money off that book. Hire a Publicist or really get a good understanding of how to be your own Publicist.

It is a good idea to hire a Publicist at least six months before your book is due to come out. The first thing your Publicist should do is read a draft of your book well before it is in print. By reading your book they will devise your campaign to match your book. If a Publicist does not read your book how can they design a campaign for the book? It requires more than just setting up interviews.

Before the book is released a good Publicist will have taken the major components from the book to start creating a dynamite media kit. This is a very important part of promoting an author (we will discuss media kits in the next chapter) without this kit doors will not open for you and your book. Most Publicists want to start pitching your book three months before the issue date, so when the book is released you are already set up to start appearing places with your newly released book.

Once you get a publishing deal or you are setup to self-published, it's when you start working on promoting the book. Do not wait until it is in print, start once you get that deal, because it's a process to getting your book out there.

There are a lot of doors you will have to knock on for book promotion and just like you got rejection when you were trying to get a publishing deal or an agent, you will get rejection from sources to promote your book. That's why it can become a full-time job to design a Marketing and Public Relations campaign. You have to remember that there are quite a few books published each year, so there are book signings, interviews and release parties going on continuously.

That's why every book store that you might want to do a book signing at might be booked and your Publicist has to work hard to set something up for your book. It takes a lot of leg work to get a book into book stores, advertise it and set-up book signings, that why it can be expensive to hire a Publicist.

How do you pay your Publicist? There are several different ways a Publicist receives payment. You can pay a set fee for a certain amount of time.

If you want an on-going marketing campaign for your book you can hire your Publicist for six months to a year to keep working on PR and Marketing for your book. If you only want to get the word out just for that newly released book, you might hire a Publicist for one to three months. It depends on you and what type of career you want as a writer.

Another way you can pay your Publicist is like an agent with a percentage of royalties from your book, which will keep them on the payroll. Most very successful writers do this because they know they will be continuing writing and selling books and they need a Publicist to continue to promote those books. Make sure when you hire a Publicist that you get what will work for your writing career and a contract for the exact length of time you need their services. That's very important when you go into a relationship with a Publicist, it's your call on how long you will need their services, and so make sure you know that before you two sign a contract.

Most people think of a Publicist as someone who is making out your schedule, writing and handling your press releases, arranging all your interviews, and setting up and attending your press junkets.

We connect that to movie stars and entertainers, because we think they are the only ones who have and need a Publicist. Does a writer need one? Yes. Writers need someone to do the same thing for them, whether they have written several books or just their first book and plan to start on a second one. A writer needs someone to manage their schedule and having your own Publicist to design a Marketing and PR campaign especially for your book is what every writer needs. They can plan your book party and set up everything so you just have to show up and have a good time.

Most importantly, they can set up and attend your book tours and be there with you, which will be a comfort. Your Publicist will generate media attention for your book from setting up radio and television interviews and coaching you on what say and how to handle those interviews. They also can write articles for magazines, newspapers on you the author and your books and arrange speaking engagements and book signings. They are the ones that will make sure everyone will know you have written a book. They also handle all the arrangements and set up your appearance dates for all your book commitments.

They care about your book as much as you do and their job is to get you and your book out there as much as possible.

Do not short change your writing career by not hiring the right professional for your writing. Now that you know what a Publicist can do, when to hire one, how to pay them and all the benefits you can reap for having one, its now time for that Publicist to actually start working for you. Your Publicist will become your friend, mentor and the person who is going to help you sell a lot of books.

But what happens if you cannot hire a Publicist because you are just getting started in your writing career? Or you have not just found the right person that you can work with to be your Publicist. Can you do it yourself? Absolutely. Sure the professional Publicist will have more contacts and actually more time to work on your PR and Marketing, but that still do not mean you can't do it yourself. Now…let's discuss the simple way you can become your own Publicist.

Becoming your own Publicist you should do the basic PR and Marketing for your book. Your very first step: after you have signed your publishing deal or signed a contract for it to be self-published, wait one month before you read your book again.

Now you are reading it from a different prospective, not as the writer, but someone who is reading a story from a business point of view to design a marketing campaign.

Remember, a Publicist designs a marketing campaign from the book, so you have to read your book to now design your campaign. This book is something that you probably have spent day and night working on, so when you do not read it for a month it is somewhat out of your system. Do not read or think about that book for one month and when you do pick it up again put your business hat on and not your writer hat.

Next step: write a short press release to your local newspaper to announce you have wrote a book, a short synopsis about the book (write what will be on the jacket cover) and the release date of publication. The press release should be who: you the author, what: your book and what's the book is about and when: the actually release date. So always keep in mind when writing your press release you are doing the: who, what and when.

When keeping this format in mind and you will never go wrong when you have to write a press release for your book. You do not want your press release to be too long and boring.

It should be just enough to catch someone attention and give certain details about the book that will make them want to go out and buy it or definitely come to your book signing.

Now that you have announced your book coming out, next you need to call small book stores in your city and book stores that are only in a fifty mile radius from your city. Do not try to set up a book signing at Barnes and Noble or any other huge book store chain. There are a lot of procedures you have to go through to get into the larger book chains, so you will get response from a small book store quicker and it's easier to do a book signing there. Also, most small books store have very loyal customers and your turn out will be much better than at a larger book chain. Calling book stores that are only fifty miles from your home will make setting up your book signing hassle free, because this is not the only thing you are doing.

The key to doing your own PR and Marketing is to make everything quick and simple, so you can keep writing and do it in the dedicated hours I suggested in the first chapter of Tuesday thru Thursday from 9:00am to 1:00pm.

Every city has a local talk show and you should book yourself on one or two of your city talk shows. Call two months before the book actually comes out and try to have a book signing date already schedule at a book store, so you can announce on the show where people can come see you and purchase your new book. Be prepared to talk about your book story and also the process of writing the book. Most interviewers want to know about you, how the book came about, where did the story come from and what you plan for you the author and your writing career in the future.

The interview with your local talk shows should be easy and your time segment will not be that long, so you should breeze through it without any problems. Just remember to focus on the book and your story.

Once you do this basic campaign and your book is out and you are generating some extra income, you are now ready to hire a Publicist. Because the professional Publicist is going to promote your book further than fifty miles from your city, get you into a major book store chains and plenty of radio and television appearances.

In the next chapter, you will learn how to do a media kit, so with the basic PR and Marketing you have done, your Publicist will be able to add what you have to the major media kit they will do to get your book out to all the media for the promotion you need and want for your new book.

So here are the simply four steps to becoming your own Publicist:

1. Read book one month after signing your deal to publish.
2. Write a short press release of whom, what, and when.
3. Set up book signing at local book stores and 50 mile radius book stores.
4. Book yourself on local talk show

Chapter Three

The Media Kit

One of the first things your Publicist will do is put together your media kit. What exactly is a media kit? The media kit will identify everything about you and your book. It is the link between you and the media and how your Publicist will set-up interviews for radio and television, get an article written on you and your book with different magazines and newspapers, and get your book into some of the major book stores.

Your media kit is a folder with all the data on you and the book you have just written. One of the reasons many newly published authors are not so successful, is they do not have the right package to provide the media or book stores with the necessary information they need to conduct an interview or place their books into the stores.

Your media kit is one of the tools that will also open the door for a writer to become known and to sell books. Why is this tool so important? It is the one thing that can sum up your entire career as a writer.

Of course when you first start out, your kit will not have that many pages in it, because this is your first book and you have not been out promoting the book to a lot of places yet. As your writing career grows, so will your media kit. Anything that is written about you and your book, you should always keep copies of everything, even your church bulletin or your company newsletter announcing your book.

There is not any announcement whether it's in a major publication or something small and unknown that you should not keep adding to your media kit. This is the first impression that media and book stores will have of you and your book.

Presentation is important with anything that we do, that's why you need a Publicist to create your media kit and not you the author just throw some information together and put it into a folder. A Publicist first and most importantly puts together these dossiers for a living. The kit not only represents you, the author, but it also represents the Publicist. How the kit is presented to a client and what's in it can make or break you.

You want your kit to be professional, attractive, along with being in an order and with all the documentation that is needed to promote you the author and your book.

Most Publicists send out media kits in attractive folders with company letterhead, along with an introductory letter. The kit will have the author's bio and photo, fact sheet, book cover photo, press releases, book excerpt, clippings from previous media interviews and articles, and testimonials or endorsements. Your media kit can also include the Q&A (questions and answers) you want someone to ask who will be interviewing you about your book. Your Publicist will gather all this information and put it into place to create your calling card that will grow and follow you throughout your writing career.

Let's talk about some of the information that goes in a media kit and why that information is important. The first thing is the author bio. Every writer needs this so the public will know who the author is.

Your bio will demonstrate why you are an expert on the subject of your book and will also show your career path from early days up to when you became an author. It clearly states your background and your accomplishments and should be between 100 to 500 words.

If this is your first book, your bio will probably be short and that's okay. As your career as a writer grows, so will your bio. The most important thing about a bio whether it's short or long is someone should be able to know who you are at that certain time in your life. Your very first bio written will probably be more about what you have been doing career wise that has lead to the career you now have as a writer. Most first books are in some way an autobiography of you the writer, because most of the time we write what we know.

A bio simply lets people know who you are and is used to introduce you when you undertake speaking engagements, and will be read before you start an interview. Along with that bio is an author photo. This is very important because your picture is used on flyers, bulletin boards, brochures and most importantly on your book cover.

When your Publicist sends out your media kit for book signings, speaking engagements and interviews that will be the picture they will use. These two documents tell the public who you are, whereas the fact sheet, the book cover, and book excerpt is what will inform the public about your book.

A fact sheet will give the details of your book by listing the title, author's name, publication date, ISBN and the number of pages in the book and it's very important to the media, especially when they are going to interview you. This gives them all the important information right at their fingertips.

The book cover photo shows what your book looks like, and the excerpt from the book shows the impact of your work. Usually the Publicist will pull some of the beginning, the middle and end of the text, so the reviewer/interviewer can get a good understanding of the content of the book.

Now that people know who you are and about your book, the next piece of information should include any reviews, press releases, testimonials and endorsements about your book.

Anything that has been said about you and your book should go into your media kit. If you have attended any conferences, speaking engagements or even a book club, make sure you get a testimonial or an endorsement from those events. It does not matter how small your press release is, or if you only spoke for thirty minutes, you still need to include that in your media kit.

In the beginning a new writer usually will not have a lot of endorsements, so that's when you have to become created. That work newsletter that was sent around announcing one of their employees has written a new book; keep a copy because that's an endorsement. Your church bulletin becomes something you can put in your media kit and even if you get an email from someone who has read your book that can become an endorsement also in the beginning.

When all this information is put into a folder a Publicist can send your media kit anywhere for any magazine or newspaper to do a story on you and your new book. You can do radio interviews from home just from a media kit that they have on you and your book, because it will give the interviewer all the information they need know.

Your Publicist may include at least ten interview questions along with the answers that will highlight the most important things about you and your book. This is very helpful to anyone interviewing you, because usually they do not have the time to read your entire book. A Publicist knows this and will do everything to make that interview go smoothly, so you the author can have a great interview and your message about your book will be well received by the public.

Your interviewer usually likes to ask for key points, tips and strategies, so your questions and answers should relate to exactly that. The first three questions should be the ones you want to be asked so you will have the time to discuss them. The key to doing questions and answers is to make the audience interested in your book so they will rush out and buy it.

It could take your Publicist several weeks to create this kit. Gathering all the documentation and putting it together takes some time, because don't forget, this will represent you and your work.

One thing a new author needs to remember is that the kit might not initially have all above information, because you are just getting started. Your bio might only be 100 words or less when you first start out, but it can expand as you become more established. A new writer's media kit might only consist of a bio, photo, book cover, book excerpt, and questions and answers. This kit will be totally different from that of an established author but as you grow, your folder will grow.

Ideally, the media kit should be available right after your publication date for the release of your book. A good Publicist will have it ready and know where to send it just as your book is coming out, so the media and book stores can be alerted as to when your book is on sale.

The media will not wait until you put a kit together; you need that kit to be assembled beforehand, so you will not miss the opportunity of an interview. Having an interview just as your book is coming out (especially if you are a new writer), is the best way to be introduced to the writing industry and the public. Your first book media kit will be small, because it's your first book and there is limited information on it.

Your next media kit for your second book and every book after will be fuller with endorsements, press releases and acknowledgements.

Why do you need a media kit? If you want to do interviews, speak at writing conferences, have a book signing at major book stores, and be feature in different magazines and newspapers, a good media kit is what will make all of that happen. This is one of the most vital items any author can have that will help to promote and profit their career as writer. It will tell anyone everything they need to know about you the writer, and the book you have written. It is the reason you will have great interviews and will be seen and heard as a writer. A beautiful folder with all this information about you will open doors to all those opportunities and more.

Now… how do you do your own media kit? First you do have to invest a small amount of money in the materials you will need to set-up your media kit. You want it to look professional and not look like someone just threw some papers in a folder.

Your first purchase should be some business cards with all your contact information on it and then you need to make a visit to your local Office Max or Office Depot store.

You need to decide on a color theme for your business items. For example, when I first started out my color theme was light blue and navy blue. I made sure I ordered my business cards in that color with my name, my title(writer) and my contact information with includes phone numbers, email and website if you have one. Then I bought a pack of business folders from Office Max with two pockets that had a business card holder on the left side of the folder. I bought the most expensive ones in a color of navy blue and I purchase some light blue paper to use for letterhead to put my short bio on. I had a friend take my picture, had it developed at my local Walgreen's and had a copy of that picture put on photo paper that I bought at Office Max also.

Next you need to type your bio on the paper you purchase. Your bio can simply be your name, where you live, and some details about your present career and try to connect that to your book you just written.

If you have any announcements of your book you can list it. Your next page should be your fact sheet with: book title, author name, publication date, ISBN and the number of pages of the book. If your media kit only has three or four pages, that's okay in the beginning because you are just getting started. The most important thing is to make sure it looks professional.

Here are your four steps to do your own media kit.
1. Order business cards
2. Take a Photo
3. Purchase very nice Business Folders
4. Do BIO and Fact Sheet

Chapter Four

Marketing Campaign

The Coca-Cola Company does it for every new Coke when it comes out, why aren't writers having it done for every new book of theirs that will be released? What does a major corporation like Coca-Cola do to get their new product out there? A marketing campaign; what every writer needs for their new book. A marketing campaign is how you'll get your book out there to the public. Each book should have a campaign designed especially for that book. This will allow it to reach the best market for that particular book.

When the Coca-Cola Company has a new drink they want to introduce, their marketing department designs a new campaign for that particular new Coke. Every time you look up you will see a new Coke commercial on TV talking about the new Coke, and when you go into the grocery store you will see a new display ad on the new Coke. This is done to catch your attention to make you want to try it.

Writers need to do the same thing with their new books; you need to have a marketing campaign for your book to make people want to go out and buy it to read.

How you market your book will decide how profitable you will be as a writer, career wise and financially. Even though when you are writing a book, you are not looking at the profits. Most writers just have something they want to say and they just want it to be published so people can read it. As a writer you should not focus on the profits of your book, but you do have to keep in mind that your book can make you money and you have to pay attention to the business side of things to become profitable.

A campaign should be designed for your new book covering everywhere your new book will be seen; all the venues where you can speak about it, book signings at different book stores, online information and even a book party to introduce it to family and friends. Getting that book out there is the main reason of your marketing campaign. Having your newly published books sitting in your house or garage is not how the public will know that your book exists. Your marketing campaign is what will get and keep your book and you the author in the public eye. It's one of the main jobs of your Publicist, to design a marketing campaign for your book.

Your Publicist has read your book and they will know exactly where to send it, and be responsible for making sure it gets there. Advance planning for marketing your book is crucial to your career. Everything from the packaging to an advanced reading copy to making sure it looks professional. Once you hire a Publicist you should immediately start working together on your marketing campaign.

When I work with writers as their Publicist, I tell them to think of me as their Wedding Planner. When you plan to get married you work on the big day months and months before you actually say 'I Do'. It's the same thing with your book; we start working on your marketing campaign months before the book comes out. You are 'engaged' to that book, just like being engaged to a significant other. While working toward being married, an author is working toward a book release. That's their marriage. The steps are pretty much the same.

After your Publicist has read your book they know exactly where they want the book to be shown and how to run the marketing campaign to get the best results. Let's say you have written a book about yoga.

Your campaign should focus on different health clubs, TV shows that have something to do with exercising/fitness, or maybe as a guest speaker at a health retreat that features yoga as part of their program. Your Publicist should work everything around that topic. Your campaign should match your book. They have to relate to each other for people to have an interest to come out to see you and hear about what you've written.

Now let's get into all the different campaigns for your book. The very first campaign should be to introduce your book right after it has been released. The best way to do that is through a book party. Having a book party to introduce your book is just like having a wedding reception to introduce your new spouse. I design my client's book release parties with themes and make it into an extravagant affair. You, the writer, have worked for years on your book and once it is released, you need to celebrate. We throw the party so family and friends can see the new book and enjoy your success. One of my favorite book parties that I have designed is Book Signing at Tiffany's.

We do the room in Tiffany blue with blue cupcakes and each guest when they sit at their table will receive a small gift in the Tiffany blue box, such as a keychain of the book cover. Even if you do not have something as elaborate as this, have some type of theme for your book party so you and your guests can enjoy and celebrate.

The next major part of the campaign is setting up speaking engagements. Getting out and talking about your book will open doors in so many different ways. Not only will you be seen and people will hear about your book, but speaking can become a second income. Hitting the speaking circuit can lead to selling more books than you might in a book store. Every time you speak somewhere your Publicist should negotiate the rights to sell your books there. This is especially good for self-published authors who are usually ignored by the major distributors that are the backbone of the publishing industry.

Once you get your feet wet as a speaker, your Publicist will be able to book you continuously at different writing conferences and any events that relate to your book topic. Along with making money from royalties, and money from book sales at speaking engagements, you will start making money from speaking fees.

Speaking engagements keep you and your book out in the public eye and will help to sell more books that in long run will make you more successful and make you a lot of money. Also when you speak at different writing conferences, you get the chance to network with other writers where they can learn something from you and you can learn something from them.

Another campaign strategy is book signings. Once your book comes out you will need to do signings at different book stores. Do not always think that you have to have book signings at all the major book stores. Small intimate book stores are also great for book signings. They usually have people who have been shopping there for years and will come out to support the store. I have had several clients who have written religious books and I have set them up for book signings at different Christian book stores, which have been a great success.

The key to having a success book signing is to have the signings somewhere that you know will draw a crowd. Perhaps you could do a reading to make people want to hear more, so they will buy the book.

Yes, we all want to get into the major stores, but do not forget about the small ones, or the specialty book stores if your book relates to that store. Tell family, friends and co-workers about your book signing and get them to attend, because the more traffic the store has for your book, the more likely they are to invite you back for future signings.

And of course, the most important marketing campaign in these days and times is all the different media sources. Everyone should take advantage of their Web sites, Twitter, Facebook and YouTube, but you also should develop a campaign for these media sources. Just don't put things out there, plan how and when you are going to announce the release of your book. Facebook is a good way to announce that you have a book that is going to be released, with the title of the book and release date. This way all your Facebook friends everywhere can go out and purchase your book. Twitter is good for tweeting each stage of your book release and where all your book signings will be. When you have a book signing and you do a reading at the book signing, have someone record it so you can put it on YouTube. This is really good for self-published authors, because you might get discovered by an agent to get a publishing deal.

The best source is a Web site; you can put a copy of your book cover, several chapters of the book and all your information where you can be contacted. You also can put your Web site address on your business cards that will go into your media kit.

Not having a marketing campaign for a book is one of the biggest mistakes new writers can make. Books need help to fly off the shelf. People have to know that the book exists, and having a marketing plan for your book is the only thing that can make that happen. There are so many new titles produced each year and you need a plan to capture the attention of the reading public.

Also, with so many writers publishing their own work it is vitally important to devise a marketing plan. You alone will be responsible for getting that book out in front of the public and into book stores. Having a marketing campaign specifically design for your book will make that happen and give you a better chance of being in different stores.

A good marketing campaign is such a key part of a writer becoming a success. You have to think of your book as a product and like any product, it's there for the consumer to purchase it. Having it published is only the beginning.

If you do not have a marketing campaign that is going to help you keep your book out in the public eye, all your hard work will be for nothing. A book party to introduce your book to family and friends is not enough to make you a success. Once every family member and friend has purchased your book (you hope!), then what? Your marketing campaign will tap into people to read rather than sitting in a box at home.

When you work with a Publicist to devise a campaign for your book, you will know that your book and you, the author, will be accessible to the public. The reason you published a book is to share a message; make sure you have a way of getting that message out there. A solid, well-planned, meticulously executed campaign will do just that.

Before you hire that Publicist here are your four steps that you can do for your own marketing campaign:

1. Throw a small intimate book party at home for family and friends.
2. Set-up a speaking engagement at your church, work and the library.
3. Set-up a book signings at your neighborhood book store.
4. Create a Web page for your new book.

Chapter Five

Book Promotions Items

No matter where you work, there are working items that you have to have to do your job productive. In an office you usually have: a desk, a computer, a phone and office supplies like pens, paper and other office supplies. These items are the things that will make you productive while working to be a success at your job. In the writing industry you also need items to be a successful author. Once you write your book and it's published, you need book promotion items. Even though you have a Publicist, they actually need items to work with to help promote you and your book.

The first thing you need to do is decide on a budget for your book promotion items and how much promotion you intend to do for your book. You do not want to have a large supply of items you have purchased, but you only plan to do a little promoting. One way to decide how much book items that you need to purchase is by deciding if this is a one book deal or you plan to become an author with several books and a career as a writer.

If you just plan on one book, than you just need the basic items, but if you are planning a long time career, you need to go all the way. Your basic book items are: author picture, picture of your book cover, newspaper release and bookmarks. These are some of the things that are in your media kit, but you can also use for book signings or mail outs.

You always need a photo of you the author and the book cover, so people can see who you are and what your book looks like. These items are really good for your book signing, whether it's at a large book store or the neighborhood book store. The press release is to announce where you will be and bookmarks of your book is always good for give away. These things do not have to be very expensive, but you also have to keep in mind that you do want quality items, especially since that's all you are having.

Now…if you have plans for a long time career as a writer, you want to have a larger budget for your book items. You have to keep in mind that you are building a brand and not just a book that was published. Building a brand means follow-up books, speaking engagements and possible even teaching classes on writing.

When I started out as writer I wrote my first romantic novel, then I started freelancing with different articles. That lead to teaching writing classes and speaking engagements, then I developed my first company Writing4Success. I was building a brand and name for myself in the writing industry, so I have a huge variety of book items to support my brand.

If you plan to build a brand, which could consist of follow up books from what you have written, you need a budget and a variety of book items. Of course you also need the basic items of your photo, picture of your book cover, newspaper release and bookmarks. Your very first important book item is business cards. As I told you earlier, have a color that you want to use for your business cards and letterhead. Your business cards should have all your contact information and you should have them on you at all times to pass out when you talk to anyone about your book.

Your next important item is a Web page especially for your book. This Web page should be for nothing but your book. Besides having the cover of your book and a few chapters on it, you should definitely have a calendar of all your events for the book.

Anyone should be able to pull up your Web site and see where you will be speaking, having book signings, teaching a class and the most important thing of when your next book be released. Passing out those business cards with your Web address and email is what will keep the public linked up to you. Speaking of email, I suggest you create an email just for your writing. This way everything pertaining to your writing will go to that email and not your personal email.

Now let's talk about some of the fun book items you should have to keep your book and your name out there. Give away are really good for promoting and if you plan a serious career as a writer you should have bookmarks, ink pens, T-shirts, mouse pads, tote bags, key chains, cups, post cards, and invitations all with your book cover on it. There will be times when you should have it all to give away and then it will be certain events that you only need to give out a few things. Remember you will have to do this for each book, but if you continue to publish books that you are making a profit off of and you can set up a budget for your book promotion items for each book.

Book promotion items are also good for putting into a media kit to send to a book store or to an organization for a speaking engagement. In the media kit that you are sending out to those two places, you can put bookmarks and a mouse pad in that media kit to your contact person, so when your event is over they will still have something visual of your book. This is good for keeping you and your book fresh on their minds when you want another engagement with them.

Your four steps to do your own book promote items are:

1. Take a photo of yourself and book cover with your phone.
2. Set up an email just for your book.
3. Get a free Web site for your book and your book announcements.
4. Order bookmarks of your book cover from somewhere like Vista Print.

Chapter Six

You Have Your Four Steps: Now Use Them

Public Relations and Marketing is the key to becoming a successful writer. In these days and times everyone, including me, is self-publishing and you need to know how to make your book become a success. Doing PR and Marketing yourself does not have to be hard if you use this book as a guideline. Even when it becomes too much with all the success you will have as an author, this book will also help you to know what to look for and expect when you hire someone to do it for you.

Every writer can use some guidance or if you are an experienced writer you can use a refresher on Public Relations and Marketing. The whole concept of this book is to show every writer know matter what you write how to do your own PR and Marketing without spending a lot of money or taking time away from your writing. Your main job as a writer is to write, but you also have other jobs in the writing industry to become a successful writer. Using the main four tools of Publicist, Media Kit, Marketing Campaign and Book Promotion Items is how you will succeed when your book is published.

Know what you want in your writing life, so you can know how to go about to get it. You have to decide if you want a career as a writer or you just have a one book in you. Determining that up front will help you to decide in what direction you need to go and what tools you need to use to accomplish that. Do take the time to think about the future of your book and not just focus on getting it published.

There is a life after publication for your book and just like in your own life you have to make decisions on what you want and how to get it.

It all starts with the Publicist, whether you become your own Publicist or hire someone. This book will help you to know what simple things you can do to be your own Publicist and also be guidance on what to expect if you hire one. Do not think that a Publicist is not needed, because this person is the one who will get and keep you and your book out in the public. Don't spend time or money on a book just to have it in print…make sure someone is going to read it.

Getting that information out there on your book comes from your media kit, so make sure you do it right, because it represent you and your book. Your media kit will be seen by so many different people that you want to make sure it's professional and informative, if not it will be defeating the purpose. Your media kit can make or break you when it comes to getting your foot into the door of all the different places you need to promote your book.

That media kit should be a key player in your marketing campaign. When you are trying to get a speaking engagement or a book signing, you or your Publicist should always send your media kit to whomever, you are trying to set up something with. It's very important to send it to the book stores for a book signing, so they will know who you are and have all the information about your book on hand. Remember a book signing is when your book is published and people are invited out for you to sign the book at a book store and you can also do a reading of some chapters out of the book.

Whereas, a book party is to announce that your book is published and you have food, wine and gifts (usually something with your book cover on it) for just family and friends.

One of your greatest marketing tools is going to be radio, TV and print. You or your Publicist should definitely try to get you on your local radio and TV talk shows once your book is published. With the right Publicist approach and the right media kit you should be having interviews about your book. Do not forget to do that press release to your newspaper and also send a press release to any local magazines in your city.

When promoting your book you are going to need some book promotion items to give out and have information on you, the book and how to contact you. It sounds like all the book promotion items can be expensive, and it can be, but it's an invest that will pay you back in the long run. There are some short cuts you can take and one of my favorite that I have been using for years is Vista Print. Once you start ordering from them you will get all types of specials and my favorite special is when they have free items and all you have to do is pay for shipping.

Every time they have free letterhead, pens, stickies pads, note pads and post cards, I order. You can't beat getting those products with your logo or name on it for free. Trust me; if you order every time they run that special, you will have a nice supply of products that you can use for your writing career.

As you can see all of this ties together, your Publicist does a Media Kit, the Media Kit is used for Marketing Campaigns, Marketing is what will get you book signings, interviews and speaking engagements and your Book Promotion Items is what you will use to promote your book.

Every writer has a story they want to tell and when you are writing most writers just want to finish the book and get it published, but you need to always think about what will happen after it's in print. There is no way around it you need Public Relations and Marketing to be successful.

Now…before I go I want to talk to you about one more thing, and that's the business side of writing. I always tell my clients that there are two sides to writing, the creative side and the business side. The creative side is the fun side where you get to just write and create your book.

The other side is the business side and it's a very important part of writing. The writing industry is a business and its run like any other business. Once you decide that you want a career as a writer you need to start setting it up as a business.

The Public Relations and Marketing side is the business side. You are not just sitting in your office all alone writing anymore. You are interacting with other business people from the media, people that work at different venues, book store managers and PR people that handle the booking at book stores to a dean at a school if you want to speak or teach writing. That's why I suggested earlier that if you are going to become your own Publicist have business hours that you work, because you will be dealing with other business people that work in their offices from 9-5.

You can't set up appointments at 11:00pm at night when you are writing in your office. Make sure you set up a schedule to work with other business people in the times that they are working.

Another business side of writing is setting your writing up as a business. I suggest you decide on a name for your writing business, so you can get an EIN number from IRS. This is the number you can use to file your taxes, and yes you will have to file taxes from any royalties from your book, speaking fees, teaching fees and any other money you make off your writing. You also will need to use that EIN number to open a business bank account to deposit any money from your writing to keep it separate from your personal account. Also, keep every receipt from any and everything that you purchase pertaining to your writing, because it can help you with your taxes.

Even though I've only given you four steps for Public Relations and Marketing, that's all it's takes if you do and follow those steps you will succeed in promoting your book and your career as a writer. All the tips of what to do from the four simple steps at the end of each chapter to the advice on setting your writing up as business are tips, strategies and advice that I have give writers now for almost ten years. When I first got in the business, I didn't know anyone to go to for advice or solutions and I had to learn by trail and error.

Now after writing myself for almost fifteen years, teaching writing for nine years, two companies later and one of my greatest accomplishment of being an international published freelance writer in Great Britain, I still love what I do.

The road to becoming a successful writer can be a hard, but with persistence and patience and The Four Steps to Public Relations and Marketing for Writers, you can do it. Good Luck!

www.ingramcontent.com/pod-product-compliance
Lightning Source LLC
Chambersburg PA
CBHW071623170526
45166CB00003B/1167